Growing with Gratitude

A Poetic Journey of Healing

Janey Colbourne

A Plantseer Press Imprint

Contents

Introduction

Growing with Gratitude is the story of my healing journey, in the form of poems I wrote along the way. It begins in a place of despair and gradually I find reasons for hope and gratitude. I hope that it may help anyone else who has experience of struggling with serious illness or disability to find hope and discover their own reasons to be positive. It is possible to find the source of inner healing, irrespective of the state of our physical health. Creative expression in any form can be highly therapeutic, so I encourage you to put pen to paper, put aside any judgements or worries about how 'good' it may be, and write for your own benefit.

The most powerful positive force through this period of my life has been the cultivation of gratitude. Gratitude for the wonderful people in my life, for nature and the Earth that sustains us, for the medical and healing treatments, and for the simplest things in everyday life. Look around and see the gifts you have. The more you look the more you see, and the more you will create.

With Gratitude to all beings who have inspired and supported me.

Janey Colbourne 2016

The Day My Garden Died

The day my garden died,
I took my heart inside
to tend no more the earth
till time had healed.

I had a beautiful herb garden, in pots, in my tiny backyard. When I became ill, I was
unable to attend to it. Slowly it deteriorated. It became symbolic of the death of my
life as I knew it, a kind of winter of the soul.

Forgetti Spaghetti

Forgetti spaghetti,
that's what this brain is made of.
Don't think twice,
memory's on strike.

What's left behind
when you've lost your mind?
Your heart, that's what.
That's what we all are made of.

Confusion reigns
inside the brain,
but the heart has its own kind of knowing.
You know it.

Anyone who had had chronic illness such as chronic fatigue, fibromyalgia, thyroid or parathyroid disease may well recognise this 'brain fog' as we call it.

Headspace

I've hit the mental wall,
don't talk to me today.
Head space is my sanctuary,
I've nothing more to say.

I discovered that solitude was respite for my weary brain.

I Call Light to Myself

Thank you Karen, friend
for bringing in the light,
the light of clarity and insight,

for reminding us,
we sit upon the Earth,
for connecting us with the seasons.

True friend of the heart,
you practise your art
for the highest good of all.

A safe space created
builds up trust,
a circle of wisdom strong.

Karen of One Heart Healing is a wise and dear friend who is skilled in meditation and healing techniques. She is an expert at discerning the deeper issues in people's lives and in supporting them to grow in their own way. I cannot overstate how much her support has helped me. In her meditation group is a circle of true and compassionate friends.

To My Parathyroid

A tiny gland,
like a grain of rice,
but you have changed my life.
With awesome power,
you did transform
my body and
my mind.

Your messages
I did not hear.
You grew so you could shout.
Pea size now,
but you're the boss,
I hear you now,
for sure.

A gift you gave,
the lessons learned,
although it did seem harsh,
you opened up new
worlds in me,
and strangely it
felt right.

You will destroy me
in the end,
so I must say goodbye.
It's hard to part,
before you go,
my gratitude
I show.

It is strange how parathyroid disease, as with any endocrine disorder, can affect your very personality. Through the changes of this illness I was forced into a new path that brought many blessings as well as challenges. I chose to take the effects of the illness as my higher self's guidance.

Indigestonion

Onion, why must you fight me so?
Battered membranes
you remind me, with frequency,
Alliums unwelcome here it seems.
Turmoil in the tract,
with sadness I concede
no longer to force a union
with an onion.

Under the Knife

I missed National Poetry day.
Never mind.
I was mending my body
and resting my mind.

I was under the knife and
facing my fear,
to reclaim my health
and freedom so dear.

To Betty

Lovely lady,
Betty who is brave,
Thank you for
your inspiration.

At peace with
the world,
and the next
adventure.

Gushing with your
gratitude,
touching all
around you.

Bless you.

Betty was a lady I met when I was in hospital. She was terminally ill and was radiating such joy, equanimity and gratitude that it was infectious. I was so touched by her courage, I gave her this poem before I left.

Opening

There's inspiration and wisdom
in every situation,
if you open
your heart and your mind.

The Counsellor

The gift you've given
cannot be undone,
the most precious thing of all.
Your time, your attention,
undivided,
holding the space
for me.

Every day a life is changed
for the better,
the world a better place,
the seeds of compassion sown,
passed on,
and on,
and on.

Your gift does not stay in this room,
although our words will do.
It spreads like sunrise,
ripples in a pond.
It radiates
through each of us,
on and on.

I had person-centred counselling with an amazing lady. I think the poem says it all.

Magic

I so love the season's change,
engaged with all my senses.
This time is charged with magic
reawakening me.

I wrote this in Autumn. Being connected to nature makes me feel so alive, and full of
gratitude.

For Poppa

Always there,
your hand to hold,
whether I feel bold
or scared.

Laughter or tears,
you have no fears
to be there
by my side.

Always safe,
but always free,
to be you
and me.

No harsh words spoke,
no judgement made,
yet truth be told,
with love.

My poppa is a true friend, someone who has always accepted me for who I am and found reasons to be proud of me, even in my most foolish times.

The Shadow

I thought I'd faced
My greatest fear
The day I went under
The knife

But no

Today I face it
Much deeper than that
The threat came from within

With courage I stand
How else could I be?
Face to face
With mortality

Look back with true sight
What I made to protect
Is not what it seems at all

What once felt safe
Is in fact a cage
A cage of bones

And now

I take up my flaming sword

I shook hands with Death
I'll see you one day
But not today

In a gust of wind

It's gone

Release

What kept you safe
Becomes a cage
Release your heart
Upon the page

Your words are now
The avenue
To make yourself
A life more true

This poem expresses my perception of my physical illness as my body's way to protect itself or compensate for unresolved issues in my life, which then became in itself a threat to me, a 'cage'. In poetry I found a sense of meaning and a way to free myself.

Healing

Regardless of
My body's state
I know I'm healed and whole

Much work was done
Courageously
Until I freed my soul

Vitality has
Fired me up
I'm feeing like I'm new

I'm having fun
Creatively
And sharing this with you

True healing of the soul, peace of mind and inner freedom, does not always have to
immediately correlate with physical health.

Mutiny in the Gland

Mutiny rears its ugly head
The cells are rebelling it seems
Recruiting for pirates
While Captain is sleeping
The sly ones
Took over the gland

You're busted
Can't trust you
You're making me sick
It's time to be walking the plank
To be frank

A little humour helps us through hard times.

The Surgeon

Under the knife
You hold a life
In balance

With courage you work
And lives transform
Of those who
Lay trust in you

Thank you

I have so much gratitude to all the staff involved in my surgery and the preparation
for it. I was treated with so much compassion, humanity and respect. And they did an
excellent job. I can only imagine the sense of awesome responsibility to hold
someone's life in your hands like this every day.

Connected

Feeling and seeing
Breathing the scent
Molecules everywhere

Open to energy
Rooted to earth
Connected everywhere

Always belonging
Always at home
Belonging everywhere

I have found the practice of grounding meditation invaluable in maintaining my sanity. Spending time in the woods really helps with this. When you feel connected to earth and nature it is so energising and strengthening.

The Tortoise

For a time
I walked beside
The tortoise
His gentle wisdom
Shared with me
Slow down
Said he

Be peaceful
Take the time
To process
Your emotion
Just listen then
Sit with it
And see

Life's too short
To rush around
Unconsciously
This paradox
We understand
Will make us
Free

In this modern world of haste, when adverts entreat us to take tablets and get back to work, slowing down and being really present in the now is a revolutionary act. Convalescence is a lost art that benefits longer term health. On a more daily basis, slowing down can help to prevent illness. I have learned not to panic and try to submerse my difficult emotions through life's distractions. Running away from our feelings doesn't heal them. Being patient and giving ourselves time to work out what our emotions are really telling us rather than acting unconsciously in haste is the way to true emotional health.

Book you are

Book you are the door
Into the mind of another
A new perspective
Wisdom is shared

Book you are the window
Into the soul of another
Connected
I see myself reflected

For a time I see through your eyes
We enter the universal mind
The sea

Reflection on the power of books and reading.

Bacteria Banishing Spell

Begone foul foe
Bacteria know
I'll pursue you
Till you're through

No hiding place
Get out my space
Your end is nigh
Goodbye

Open to receive

I am as a cup
An opening bud
Ready to receive
The light
The waters clear
And sparkling

I think at this point I was really starting to feel the benefit of regular meditation.

For the Love of Lentils

Lovely lentils,
lenticular form,
Soothing to stomach
and heart.
Tiny packaged vitality,
a gift of wellbeing
within.

Lentils are a wonderful food, especially good for our gut health. They encourage our friendly gut flora and are a cheap and environmentally friendly source of protein. I craved them after surgery. Sometimes cravings do tell us what we really need.

My love is

My love is the rising sap
The heartbeat of trees
The blood of the Earth
Arises in me

My love is the place
Where Earth touches air
Where sunlight and
Waterfall mingle

A love poem to Nature. I wrote this standing on a bridge over the river in the woods,
looking down into the water.

Verdant heart

Verdant heart
So filled with bliss
The ripening bud
And nature's kiss

Align with trust
Releasing soul
Ecstatic love
Now feeling whole

To my suffering

If it hadn't been for you
I would never have seen
What I needed to do
To be true

You broke me
Remoulded me
Cast me anew

Now I see with my heart
It's true

A final note of gratitude for the journey that has brought so much personal growth.

Burnout: A collective responsibility

Burnout. It happens even to the kindest, warmest hearted people. In fact they are possibly the most vulnerable to it. Those in the caring professions: nurses, doctors, teachers, social workers. Those with caring responsibilities at home. What do I mean by burnout? When your energy is sapped and stretched to the limit. When demands exceed your capacity. When you have no time for you, to replenish yourself. When you put others before yourself so often you are in danger of making yourself ill. When you feel that you have no choice but to carry on, everyone else's needs are so important. You might not see the early warning signs. You build a hard but brittle shell around your psyche. You begin to get impatient, irritable. You begin to not care. The shell starts to crack. When you're surprised to find you hate your job that you once put your heart and soul into, when it feels like everyone wants a piece of you, when you begin to turn upon the very people you wanted to help, then it has gone too far.

We are so fortunate in the UK to have free healthcare, social services and free education for our children. Ok well not technically free, although free at the point of access; we pay for it through taxation and we have the right to expect a decent standard of care and respect. On the other hand, when not required to hand over cash on delivery, does this lead to a sense of entitlement? Does it lead to an undervaluing of the effort of professionals? We know those professionals are paid, in some cases handsomely, while others graft for little pay but with great devotion. Family members care for each other with no expectation of pay or reward. In a materialist culture, when money exchange does not take place, do we value the effort of those who serve us? In traditional societies healers may give care without demanding payment, but gratitude is always given. Some form of exchange takes place. Both parties benefit from this.

Should we assume that because someone is paid by the state, we do not owe them anything? A simple "thank you so much for your time" costs us nothing but gives much in return. A value that makes the job worthwhile. A few words that show we do not take them for granted. A direct and personal exchange of energy, that in fact is nourishing to both. Gratitude is awesomely transformative to the giver and receiver.

This applies not only in the caring professions but in all walks of life, across all generations.

Gratitude makes the world a softer, kinder place. It softens that brittle shell of defense. There is always something to be grateful for. Even when your care has not been all that you had hoped for, there is something, some spark of effort, of love, of time that someone has put in for you. Behind that air of professionalism is a vulnerable, fallible human just like you.

What of those who are burning out? This works for them too. To remember gratitude. To look for things to be grateful for every day. To be thankful for patients, students or customers whose need gives us our job, who teach us as much as we teach them, who challenge us to be better people, whose own courage and strength is humbling. For supportive colleagues and family. Gratitude even to our own bodies and minds for the work we have done, and also even for the urgent messages of breakdown that tell us when we have had enough. Gratitude alone is not always enough. Carers need care also, and rest. Rest without guilt or pressure. The helper needs to know when to ask for help. Even healers get sick. In this modern world we have high expectations of ourselves and each other. The pressure is on, even for those who are ill.

"No time to be ill, take a pill."

How about a big dose of compassion.

Janey Colbourne 2016

Also by Janey Colbourne:

See with Heart: a collection of poems and photographs

Published by Plant Seer Press 2015

Full colour paperback available from Amazon

ebook available from:

Amazon Kindle Store

iBooks

Smashwords, Kobo and and major ebook sellers

20807118R00021

Printed in Great Britain
by Amazon